Scroogissimo

By Charly Chiarelli and Ryan M. Sero

Scroogissimo

Scroogissimo is a comedy based on the Charles Dickens classic *A Christmas Carol*. It is set in the North End of Hamilton, Ontario, where 10,000 Sicilians settled after World War II – almost all of them from the town of Racalmuto. Scrooge is "Ebenezu Scroogi", a character created by Charly (Calogero) Chiarelli. Charly is known across Canada and internationally for *Cu'fu* and *Mangiacake,* one-man plays about growing up Sicilian in the North End of Hamilton, Ontario.

Scroogi is haunted by his old partner Marley, who sends three ghosts (played by women in this version) to teach him compassion. Tiny Tim is a ventriloquist dummy, operated by Bob Cratchit, and Scroogi's housekeeper is a classic panto Dame. As performed at Artword Artbar in Hamilton, the show is chock-a-block with Christmas songs.

Artword Theatre is the creation of Judith Sandiford (Managing Director) and Ronald Weihs (Artistic Director). They operated a highly successful theatre in downtown Toronto for twelve years. In 2008, they moved to Hamilton, where they operate **Artword Artbar**, a popular live-music and performance venue in the James Street North arts district, and continue to produce, write and direct original Canadian theatre.

Scroogissimo

By Charly Chiarelli and Ryan M. Sero
based on *A Christmas Carol* by Charles Dickens

As performed by the Artword Theatre Ensemble
Script development by Ronald Weihs

Artword Press
Hamilton Ontario, 2018

First published in 2018 by
Artword Press
166 Prospect Street South
Hamilton, Ontario
Canada. L8M 2Z4

© Ryan Sero and Charly Chiarelli, 2013, 2018.

All rights reserved. Requests to reproduce the text in whole or in part should be addressed to the publisher.

Application for performance in any medium should be addressed to:
Artword Theatre
166 Prospect Street South
Hamilton, Ontario
Canada. L8M 2Z4

ISBN: 978-0-9920096-1-8

Scroogissimo

By Charly Chiarelli and Ryan M. Sero
based on *A Christmas Carol* by Charles Dickens

As performed by the Artword Theatre Ensemble
Script development by Ronald Weihs

Scroogissimo was first produced by Artword Theatre at Artword Artbar, 15 Colbourne Street, Hamilton Ontario, December 3 to 15, 2013. It was remounted at Artword Artbar in 2014, 2016 and 2018 with the same cast, except for the musician.

Direction and dramaturgy by Ronald Weihs

Produced and designed by Judith Sandiford.

Assistant Director	Paula Grove
Stage Manager	Judith Sandiford
Puppet creation	Melanie Skene

Performed by the Artword Theatre Ensemble:

Charly Chiarelli	Ebenezu Scroogi (a crusty North Ender)
Pamela Gardner	Fundraiser, Holly (Ghost of Past), Catherine (Fred's wife)
Paula Grove	Fundraiser, Little Singer, Fezziwiggi moll, Belle, Natalia (Ghost of Present)
Valeri Kay	Fundraiser, Fezziwiggi, Mrs. Cratchit, Ghost of Future
Jon-Gordon Odegaard	Bob Cratchit (and Tiny Tim), Fezziwiggi's security, Charwoman
Jay Shand	Fred (Scroogi's nephew), Ghost of Marley, Fezziwiggi's security, Pawnbroker
Music	Jennifer Lockman (2013) Tim Nijenhuis (2014, 2016) Alex Tomowich (2018)

Preface

The idea for *Scroogissimo* came about in a conversation that Judith Sandiford and I had with Charly Chiarelli in the spring of 2013. We were looking for a Christmas show for December. Charly suggested *A Christmas Carol*.

Charly grew up in Hamilton's North End, at that time inhabited largely by Sicilians, most of them from a single town, Racalmuto. He moved to Kingston where every year there was a big community production of *A Christmas Carol*. For ten years Charly played a street singer. "I had one line, but after ten years, I know all the other lines."

Artword Artbar is a block away from where Charly grew up. Ron said, "Why not do our own version here? A North End Sicilian version."

Charly gave us a sample of some of Scrooge's lines, North End style, and Ron and Judith were soon aching with laughter. Charly has great affection foe the dialect of English spoken by his Sicilian father and mother. Charly "translated" all Scrooge's speeches into North End Sicilian English. He dictated them over the phone to Judith, who tried to figure out how to spell words like "umbaggo" (humbug). And so a new North End Sicilian named Ebenezu Scroogi came to life.

Meanwhile, Ron had casually mentioned to Ryan Sero, Hamilton playwright and a member of the Artword Ensemble, that Ryan might be interested in writing the script. Ryan replied, "Be careful what you wish for." He got to work twisting Dickens's carefully crafted situations and characters into his own brand of comedy, while still preserving the spirit and social critique of the Dickens original.

Then Charly got back in, working on the script with Ryan. And once in rehearsal, the actors made their own contributions to the script. And there I was, doing my best to herd all those krazy kats and make a play.

I'm very pleased with the result, and that it came out of such a fertile collaborative process. I hope you like *Scroogissimo* as much as I do.

Ronald Weihs, Artword Theatre, November, 2018

Photos

Photos used in this playscript are from the 2016 production.
All photos by Ronald Weihs.

Cover:	Charly Chiarelli, Paula Grove
Back Cover:	Top Left: Valeri Kay, Jon-Gordon Odegaard
	Top Right: Pamela Gardner
	Bottom: Left: Charly Chiarelli, Jay Shand
Page 3:	Valeri Kay, Paula Grove
Page 6:	Valeri Kay, Pamela Gardner, Paula Grove
Page 8:	Jay Shand, Charly Chiarelli
Page 10:	Paula Grove
Page 11:	Jon-Gordon Odegaard
Page 13:	Charly Chiarelli, Jay Shand
Page 15:	Jay Shand, Charly Chiarelli
Page 18:	Charly Chiarelli, Jay Shand
Page 22:	Pamela Gardner, Charly Chiarelli
Page 23:	Charly Chiarelli, Pamela Gardner
Page 25:	Pamela Gardner, Charly Chiarelli
Page 26:	Jon-Gordon Odegaard, Paula Grove, Valeri Kay, Jay Shand, Pamela Gardner, Charly Chiarelli
Page 27:	Paula Grove, Valeri Kay, Jay Shand, Charly Chiarelli
Page 29:	Jon-Gordon Odegaard, Tim Nijenhuis, Paula Grove, Valeri Kay, Charly Chiarelli, Jay Shand, Pamela Gardner
Page 31:	Charly Chiarelli, Paula Grove
Page 32:	Charly Chiarelli
Page 33:	Paula Grove, Charly Chiarelli
Page 34:	Charly Chiarelli, Paula Grove
Page 36:	Jon-Gordon Odegaard
Page 37:	Valeri Kay, Jon-Gordon Odegaard
Page 40:	Valeri Kay, Jon-Gordon Odegaard
Page 42:	Jon-Gordon Odegaard, Valeri Kay, Pamela Gardner, Jay Shand
Page 43:	Paula Grove, Charly Chiarelli
Page 46:	Valeri Kay, Charly Chiarelli
Page 47:	Jay Shand, Valeri Kay, Charly Chiarelli
Page 48:	Jay Shand, Jon-Gordon Odegaard
Page 50:	Charly Chiarelli
Page 52:	Paula Grove
Page 53:	Charly Chiarelli
Page 54:	Charly Chiarelli, Jon-Gordon Odegaard, Jay Shand, Valeri Kay, Paula Grove, Pamela Gardner
Page 56:	Jon-Gordon Odegaard, Charly Chiarelli
Page 57:	Jay Shand, Valeri Kay, Pamela Gardner, Paula Grove, Jon-Gordon Odegaard, Charly Chiarelli

Scroogissimo

By Charly Chiarelli and Ryan M. Sero
based on *A Christmas Carol* by Charles Dickens

Characters in order of appearance:

Carollers, Narrators, Chorus

Ebenezu Scroogi

Bob Cratchit

Fundraisers

Nephew Fred

Little Girl

Marley's Ghost

Ghost of Christmas Past (Holly)

Luigi Fezziwiggi

Belle

Ghost of Christmas Present (Natalia)

Mrs. Cratchit

Tiny Tim

Catherine, Fred's Wife

Guests at Fred's Party

Ignorance and Want (puppets)

Ghost of Christmas Future

Pawnbroker

Charwoman

Act I

1. Prologue

Note: When the actors are narrating the story and functioning as an ensemble, they are identified as Narrators 1, 2, 3 and 4. The assignment of the lines is up to the director.

(Actors enter through audience singing carols. They invite the audience to join in.)

Silver Bells
Deck the Halls
Angels We Have Heard On High

(When the carol singing is finished, one of the actors says...)

NARRATOR 3. Here we go!

(The company sings a jaunty tune with no words.)

> *Lu lu lu lu lulu*
> *Lu lu lu lu luuu*
> *Lu lu lu lu lulu (etc.)*

NARRATOR 1. Marley was dead, to begin with. There is no doubt whatever about that. The register of his burial was signed by the clergyman, the clerk, the butcher, the baker, the candlestick maker, the undertaker, the chief mourner... (*he puts on dark glasses and adopts a menacing air*) ... and five brothers well connected in the community.

NARRATOR 3. Scroogi signed it. And Scroogi's name was good upon exchange for anything he chose to put his hand to.

NARRATOR 1. Old Marley was as dead as a doornail.

NARRATOR 4. (*To Narrator 1*) What's so dead about doornails?

NARRATOR 1. I don't know.

NARRATOR 4. Then why'd you say it?

NARRATOR 1. It's an expression.

NARRATOR 5. As dead as a coffin-nail would be better.

NARRATOR 2. Hang on! How is a coffin-nail more dead than a doornail? Just because a coffin-nail is in a casket doesn't mean it would be any more dead than a doornail.

NARRATOR 4. A coffin's not a casket.

NARRATOR 3. What?

NARRATOR 5. What's the difference?

NARRATOR 4. Coffins have got eight sides, a casket's only got the four.

NARRATOR 2. (*To audience*) But the real point is that a nail in either one would be better suited to a morbid metaphor than a doornail.

NARRATOR 4. It's not a metaphor.

NARRATOR 3. What?

NARRATOR 4. It's a simile.

NARRATOR 5. We're all missing the point! The POINT is that, EMPHATICALLY, Marley is DEAD!

NARRATOR 5. We're hammering this home because...

NARRATOR 4. Ah! Hammering! Nail jokes!

NARRATOR 5. We're making good on this point because otherwise, nothing wonderful will come of the story I am about to relate. If we were not perfectly convinced that Hamlet's father died before the play began, there would be nothing more remarkable in his taking a stroll at night upon his own ramparts than there would be in any other middle-aged gentleman rashly turning out after dark in a breezy spot...

NARRATOR 4. (*In a ghostly voice*) Mark me!

NARRATOR 3. Oh! We're never going to start this show!

NARRATOR 2. Who are you?

NARRATOR 4. The Ghost of Hamlet's Father! I must be avenged!

NARRATOR 2. Get out of here, you! This is *Scroogissimo*, not *Hamlet*.

GHOST (Narrator 4). Oh. Sorry.

2. Christmas eve

NARRATOR 3. Once upon a time, of all the good days in the year, on Christmas Eve, Old Ebenezu Scroogi sat busy in his counting-house.

CHRISTMAS IS A-COMING

Sing in unison:

> *Christmas is coming, the goose is getting fat*
> *Please put a penny in the old man's hat*
> *If you haven't got a penny, a ha'penny will do*
> *If you haven't got a ha'penny, then God bless you!*

Sing as a round

> *Christmas is coming, the goose is getting fat*
> *Please put a penny in the old man's hat*
> *If you haven't got a penny, a ha'penny will do*
> *If you haven't got a ha'penny, then God bless you!*

The song continues as an instrumental.

Cratchit enters and sets the stage as Scroogi's office. Scroogi has a high pedestal as a desk and a tall chair. Cratchet has a tiny desk and low stool. He sets his laptop on his desk. Then he decorates the office with Christmas garlands.

NARRATOR 3. It was cold, bleak, biting weather. The fog came pouring in at every chink and keyhole, and was so dense without, that although the court was of the narrowest, the houses opposite were mere phantoms...

NARRATOR 4. (*Ghostly voice.*) Did you say phantoms...?

NARRATORS. Stop that!

NARRATOR 4. Sorry...

Scroogi enters the office. The music changes and becomes ominous. Scroogi tears down the garlands and throws them in a trash can. He opens his briefcase and starts to count his money. He takes Cratchit's little table and puts his briefcase on it. He takes Cratchit's chair for his feet.

Three Fundraisers enter.

FUNDRAISER 1. Have I the pleasure of addressing Mr. Scroogi or Mr. Marley?

Scroogi hurriedly closes his briefcase, hiding his money.

FUNDRAISER 2. It says Scroogi and Marley on the door.

FUNDRAISER 3. Which are you?

SCROOGI. Marley, he's-a no here.

FUNDRAISER A. Will you be expecting him back soon?

SCROOGI. He die seven years ago dis-a very night. If he do, it gonna be big surprise.

FUNDRAISER 3. No doubt his liberality is well represented by his surviving partner.

SCROOGI. Liberality, conservatality, NDP-ality... I don't vote. I don't vote.

FUNDRAISER 1. You misunderstand. At this festive season of the year, Mr. Scroogi, it is more than usually desirable...

FUNDRAISER 2. ... that we should make some slight provision for the poor...

FUNDRAISER 3. ... and destitute.

SCROOGI. Eh? Whatsa matta? Day no got-a no jail on-a Barton Street?

FUNDRAISER 3. Well, of course, that is still standing.

SCROOGI. And-a welfare? Dey no give-a money to people who no deserve-a money?

FUNDRAISER 3. You have a unique understanding of the policy.

FUNDRAISER 2. Welfare, such as it is, still provides some meagre comfort to those in need.

SCROOGI. So... (*puzzled*) there's-a da jail... and-a da welfare... Ah! I got it! Dere's-a no soup kitchen or food-a bank!

FUNDRAISER 1. No.

SCROOGI. So, they closa da soup kitchen?

FUNDRAISER 1. No, I meant, "No, there are still soup kitchens and food banks."

ACT ONE 7

SCROOGI. You see? It's-a people like you the reason why I take-a so long to learn-a dis stupid-a language!

But it's-a good, yes? At-a first, I tink-a dey no got-a dis-a stuff. I am glad dey got-a, so poor lazy people no got-a come-a to my door.

FUNDRAISER 3. Sir! In the spirit of Christmas, we are trying to offer alternatives to prisons, as these scarcely furnish Christian cheer of mind or body to the poor.

SCROOGI. You got-a no chairs?

FUNDRAISER. (*both together*) CHEER!

SCROOGI. You mean like Oshkeweewee?

FUNDRAISER 3. Not that! It's a different kind of cheer!

FUNDRAISER 2. The kind you eat and drink.

SCROOGI. You eat and drink-a da chair? I telll-a you it's a stupid-a language.

FUNDRAISER 1. We are collecting money from the wealthy that we might provide the less fortunate with some meat and drink and means of warmth. We choose this time because it is a time, of all others, when Want is keenly felt, and Abundance rejoices.

FUNDRAISERS. (*Sing*) Feed the world...

FUNDRAISER 1. What shall I put you down for?

SCROOGI. You no put-a me down.

FUNDRAISER 1. You wish to remain anonymous?

SCROOGI. You no call-a me rinocerous! I like-a for you to leave me alone-a. In Chrissimiss I no look-a to be merry and I no wanna make-a lazy people merry. I pay tax-a for welfare and ever'ting-a. Is-a cost-a lots-a tax-a. For me is-a finish for poor people. Dey got-a go to welfare.

FUNDRAISER 2. Some would rather die.

SCROOGI. Okay, if-a dey like-a to die, den let-a die. Make-a da population more small – too much-a people, anyway. Look, scuzza, dis-a stuff, I no understand-a. No more talk, good-a bye.

FUNDRAISERS. (*Sing*) Feed the world...

FRED has entered and joins in. CRATCHIT joins in.

FRED. Merry Christmas, Uncle Ebenezu!

SCROOGI. Bah! Umbaggo!

FRED. Christmas? A humbug? I don't think you mean that.

SCROOGI. Eh? Merry Chrissimissi! You no got-a no right-a to be merry. That's-a fu shu'.

FRED. Oh, because you think I'm poor enough.

SCROOGI. You no just-a poor enough, you poor too much.

FRED. Well, uncle, you ought to be merry; you're rich enough.

SCROOGI. Rich enough? It's-a no thing-a! You cannot-a be rich enough. Bah, umbaggo!

FRED. Don't be so angry.

SCROOGI. "Merry Chrissimissi!" For-a you Chrissimissi time is just-a to spend lots-a money you no got-a. You become one year more old, but-a no even one penny more rich. If I got-a power to make-a happen, I  take-a da Chrissimissi tree right out-a you home, wit-a da ornaments and everyt'ing-a, and I would-a shove it right up-a you...!

FRED. That seems a trifle cruel.

SCROOGI. Eh, nephew, you keep Chrissimiss in-a you way and I keep in-a my way.

FRED. But you don't keep it.

SCROOGI. Allora, it's-a for me to leave everyt'ing alone. Even for you it's-a no good. It's-a never do any good for you.

FRED. Well, uncle, Christmas has not done me good as you would think it.

Music: A revival hymn.

Fred begins to preach, gradually becoming more impassioned.

ACT ONE 9

FRED. But, Christmas, in spite of and because of its sacred origin, is a kind, forgiving, charitable, pleasant time; the only time I know of, when men and women seem by one consent to open their shut-up hearts freely, and to think of people below them as if they really were fellow men, and not another race of creatures entirely. And therefore, uncle, though it has never put a scrap of gold or silver in my pocket, I believe that it has done me good, and will do me good. And I say, God bless it!

CRATCHIT. Bravo! Amen!

SCROOGI. (*To Cratchit.*) Whats-a all-a dis "Bravo! Bravissimo!"!? If-a you make-a one more noise, you no gonna have a job-a no more.

CRATCHIT. You're on your own, Fred.

SCROOGI. (*To Fred*) Eh, nephew, you got-a lots-a potente, power, when-a you speak. Why you no start your own church-a and make-a lots money?

FRED. Come and eat with me and Catharine tomorrow.

SCROOGI. Not even if you pay me. Why you marry a mangiacake?

FRED. Because I fell in love.

SCROOGI. Because you fall-a in love. Amore is like-a Chrissimiss: all umbaggo! Good-a bye.

FRED. You never came before I was in love. Why use it as a reason not to come now?

SCROOGI. Good-a bye!

Organ music.

FRED. I am sorry, with all my heart, to find you so resolute. We have never had any quarrel, to which I have been a party. But I have made the trial in homage to Christmas, and I'll keep my Christmas humour to the last. So A Merry Christmas, uncle!

SCROOGI. Good-a bye!

FRED. And a happy new year!

SCROOGI. GOOD-A BYE!

FRED. Merry Christmas, Bob.

CRATCHIT. Merry Christmas, Fred.

Fred exits.

SCROOGI. And here another crazy man. And-a dis-a crazy man, he work-a for me. You job-a is-a no bona job-a. Pay is-a just-a little money. You got-a wife-a, famiglia, and-a Chrissimissi time make-a you even more poor. Everyt'ing is-a so crazy, is-a make-a me crazy!

LITTLE GIRL. (*singing*)

> *God rest ye merry gentlemen,*
> *Let nothing you dismay,*
> *Remember Christ, our Saviour,*
> *Was born on Christmas Day,*
> *To save us all from Satan's power,*
> *When we were gone astray,*
> *O tidings of comfort and joy,*
> *Comfort and joy,*
> *O tidings of comfort and joy*

SCROOGI. Again, with-a the singing and the singing! All the time with-a the Chrissimissi! Bah, umbaggo!

LITTLE GIRL. (*singing*)

In Bethlehem, in Israel,
This blessed Babe was born,
And laid within a manger,
Upon this blessed morn,
The which his mother Mary,
Did nothing take in scorn,
O tidings of comfort and joy,
Comfort and joy,
O tidings of comfort and joy.

From God, our Heavenly Father,
A blessed angel came...

SCROOGI. Ehi Kid! How old you be?

LITTLE GIRL. Eight.

SCROOGI. Eight Theres-a no Santa Claus.

Little Girl starts crying and exits.

ACT ONE   11

SCROOGI. Mamma mia! Madonna! I waste-a all-a dis time!

CRATCHIT. I was going to say, "See you tomorrow", but I suppose I won't, will I?

SCROOGI. Why? You come-a to work without your glasses tomorrow?

CRATCHIT. Well... tomorrow is Christmas Day, Mr. Scroogi.

CRATCHIT. So...

CRATCHIT. It's a traditional holiday, Mr. Scroogi... so...

SCROOGI. So I gonna guess-a. Tomorrow you like-a to have-a da whole-a day off. Is-a right?

CRATCHIT. If it's quite convenient, sir.

SCROOGI. No, is-a no conveniente. and-a is-a no fair. If-a you work and I no pay you, you tink-a is-a no fair. But if-a you no work-a for one day and-a I gotta pay just-a da same, you think-a dats good?

CRATCHIT. If I work tomorrow, you'd have to pay overtime, anyway.

SCROOGI. Well, dat's-a true. You not stupido like-a you look, Cratchit.

CRATCHIT. And it's only one day a year.

SCROOGI. Oh, but you not so smart, either. You make-a scuzza for to pick-a my pocket when-a come-a December twenty-five. Okay, okay, so you got-a take off-a one-a day. But next day you got-a come-a to work-a more early, capisce?

CRATCHIT. Agreed.

SCROOGI. Is agree, is agree... what's-a dis world come-a to?

Cratchit exits.

NARRATOR 1. And so Scroogi's clerk raced off home, where he would play at Blindman's Bluff with his family...

NARRATOR 2. ... and begin the celebration of Christmas Day with the celebration of Christmas Eve, much looked forward to in the Cratchit household.

NARRATOR 3. Scroogi took his melancholy dinner in his usual melancholy tavern, and having beguiled the rest of the evening with his banker's book, went home to bed. He lived in chambers, which had once belonged to his deceased partner, Jacob Marley.

NARRATOR 4. The building was old now, and dreary. Nobody lived in it but Scroogi.

Marley, wearing a long coat, stands stiffly, becoming a door. His fist is the doorknob.

NARRATOR 3. Now it is a fact, that there was nothing at all particular about the knocker on the door of this house, except that it was very large.

NARRATOR 4. And yet Scroogi, having his key in the lock of the door, saw in the knocker, not a knocker, but Marley's face.

NARRATOR 2. Marley's face, with a dismal light about it, like a bad lobster in a dark cellar.

NARRATOR 1. Mobster?

NARRATOR 2. Lobster.

Scroogi examines Marley's face, moving it like a door knocker.

SCROOGI. Jacob Marley... Wha-? What's-a dis then, eh?

ACT ONE   13

Scroogi examines Marley's face, moving it like a door knocker.

SCROOGI. Umbaggo!

Grasping Marley's fist, he opens the Marley-door and walks past. Marley exits.

NARRATOR 2. Up Scroogi went, not caring a button for its being very dark.

NARRATOR 1. Darkness is cheap, and Scroogi liked it.

NARRATOR 3. But the phantom at the door of his long-dead partner Marley had unnerved him.

NARRATOR 1. He decided to conduct a search of his rooms before retiring for the night.

NARRATOR 2. Watch out for the fire pokers.

A crashing noise.

NARRATOR 1. And the dishes.

Sound of dishes breaking.

NARRATOR 2. And the neighbour's cat that snuck in through the upstairs window that won't close right, but that you're too cheap to fix.

SCROOGI. I don't see-a no cat.

NARRATORS. Look be*hind* you!

SCROOGI. What?

He turns and takes a step. Sound of a yowling cat.

NARRATOR 4. Scroogi continued to search. Under the table.

NARRATOR 1. Watch your head!

Scroogi bangs his head, with accompanying sound.

NARRATOR 2. Under the sofa.

NARRATOR 3. In his dressing-gown.

NARRATOR 4. You're suspicious of your dressing gown?

SCROOGI. It-a hang around look-a suspicious.

NARRATOR 1. You put it there.

SCROOGI. I did-a no such ting-a. I got-a da housekeeper.

NARRATOR 1. Big spender.

SCROOGI. You make-a fun-a me? Who are-a you peoples, anyway? Get out-a here! You got-a no business in my house!

NARRATORS. We're narrating.

SCROOGI. You gonna be narrat'-a in the jail! I'm a-going to call-a da polici!

NARRATOR 3. Look, this isn't for you.

NARRATOR 4. It's for the edification of those watching.

SCROOGI. I no take-a vacation. I work all-a time. I got it up to here with-a your bump-a my head and-a smash-a my plates, and a-step on-a da cat! I not do none of dis-a stuff until you peoples come in here!

NARRATOR 1. You're the one who tripped.

SCROOGI. You make-a me trip!

NARRATOR 1. It's really a chicken-and-egg sort of...

SCROOGI. I no eat-a chicken, egg. I eat-a polenta. All-a you! Out! Out!

The Narrators exit, grumbling and muttering.

SCROOGI. Dat's-a better. Leave an old man to eat his polenta in peace!

Weird music.

SCROOGI. Who's-a there!? What's-a dis!?

Weird music.

MARLEY. Ebenezu!

SCROOGI. That's-a me.

MARLEY. Ebenezu!

SCROOGI. You say that already.

ACT ONE   15

MARLEY. Don't you know me?

SCROOGI. I got-a take a more close-a look. You look-a like my door knocker.

MARLEY. Your door knocker looks like me.

SCROOGI. Who are you? You come-a to clean the ducts?

Weird music ends.

MARLEY. Not specifically. But I'd give you a good rate.

SCROOGI. I don't need-a no duct work.

MARLEY. Too bad, I could use the money…

SCROOGI. You a beggar, like-a da rest!

MARLEY. Oh, no! I'm not like the rest, I'm more expensive!

SCROOGI. I no like-a da sound a dat.

MARLEY. That's too bad; it feels worse than it sounds. Say! Do you like the sound of this?

Marley mimes taking some coins out of his pocket. He puts his hat on the ground, and flips a coin into it, accompanied by appropriate sounds.

SCROOGI. Money? Sure! I like-a the sound of money!

MARLEY. You try.

Scroogi and Marley take turns tossing coins into the hat.

SCROOGI. This is-a fun!

MARLEY. Say, I'm out of coins. You mind if I borrow a few?

SCROOGI. Sure, sure!

MARLEY. Thanks.

Scroogi mimes giving him some coins. Marley puts them in his pocket.

SCROOGI. Hey! What are you, a wise guy? You trick-a me for my money?

MARLEY. It's no trick! Now I'm going to clean the ducts.

SCROOGI. I don't-a got-a no ducts. I got-a hens.

MARLEY. I got a pair of hens myself. They match my pair of feet.

SCROOGI. I don't-a want a parafeet; always squawking.

MARLEY. This conversation is for the birds, you know that?

SCROOGI. What's-a matta you? Why you come-a to me? What-a you want?

MARLEY. Much.

SCROOGI. Much-a he say. I don't have much-a to give.

MARLEY. You have, but you choose not to give it.

SCROOGI. You take already!

MARLEY. Right, but you didn't *choose* to.

SCROOGI. Who you be?

MARLEY. Ask me who I was.

SCROOGI. Okay, who you was? You particulare for an illusione.

MARLEY. I'm sorry, it's just rude. You can't ask a ghost who he is, it's impolite.

SCROOGI. You gonna tell me who you was or no?

MARLEY. In life, I was Marley.

Narrators enter singing "One Love".

No! Not that Marley. Jacob Marley, your partner.

Narrators exit.

SCROOGI. Jacobi! Jacobi Marley! Hey! You look-a good.

MARLEY. Thank you.

SCROOGI. I mean, you-a dead and everyt'ing-a, but you…uh…have you lost weight?

MARLEY. A little, yes.

SCROOGI. I can see. You get a lot of exercise?

ACT ONE   17

MARLEY. I walk a lot.

SCROOGI. Being dead suits you.

MARLEY. Oh, stop. You're just saying that.

SCROOGI. No, I mean it. I mean, you a little pale, but who's no pale these days?

MARLEY. I did get a little tan last June.

SCROOGI. Yeah?

MARLEY. I was haunting a place down in Kingston.

SCROOGI. That must have been nice.

MARLEY. It's a nice little town.

SCROOGI. Oh! Where are my manners!? Sit. Can you sit?

MARLEY. Oh, yes. Of course.

SCROOGI. Well, do it, do it! Have a seat.

Music: Love's Old Sweet Song

Tell me, how you been?

Marley sits.

MARLEY. Not so good.

SCROOGI. What happened?

MARLEY. I died.

SCROOGI. Oh...!

MARLEY. Don't you remember?

SCROOGI. Well, now that you mention it, you no move too much last time I see you.

MARLEY. I was pretty sick.

SCROOGI. Was bad?

MARLEY. Terminal.

SCROOGI. Dats-a pretty bad.

MARLEY. You're telling me.

18 SCROOGISSIMO

SCROOGI. You hold up alright now.

MARLEY. Are you kidding? I'm a spectre.

SCROOGI. You a 'specter? What-a you inspect? You inspect-a da restaurants? It's a good-a job.

MARLEY. No, I'm a dead guy.

SCROOGI. Ded guy? No! You-a dis guy!

MARLEY. You know, with your kind of intelligence, I'm amazed you don't fall down more.

SCROOGI. Fall down-a more what? You make-a no sense.

MARLEY. When I was alive I made dollars.

SCROOGI. That's-a right... But you a ghost now.

MARLEY. That's what I've been trying to tell you!

SCROOGI. It's-a all umbaggo, anyway.

MARLEY. You think you're imagining things?

SCROOGI. That's-a right. I no believe.

MARLEY. But you can see me and hear me.

SCROOGI. No, no! Here me, there you!

MARLEY. You can touch me!

(Scroogi reaches out his hand. Marley slaps it away.)

MARLEY. Don't touch me!

SCROOGI. That hurt-a my hand!

MARLEY. See? Why do you doubt your senses?

ACT ONE 19

SCROOGI. Because everyt'ing-a she's affet-a my sens. Sometimes I go to mangiacake restaurant, I get-a hot beef, mash potato. You got-a to do more wit-a gravy than grave.

MARLEY. So! That's the kind of joke you're going to tell?

SCROOGI. You see dis-a toot-a pick? I just-a got-a swalla dis-a toot-a pick-a and-a so much-a ghost-a gonna come! Bah umbaggo!

MARLEY. You know, you're starting to make me mad.

Marley turns to leave.

SCROOGI. Madonna! You horrible ghost-a. Why you give-a me trouble?

MARLEY. Look here! Do you believe in me or not?

SCROOGI. Okay, okay, I believe. Why you come-a to me? Minchia!

Music: ominous, in a minor key.

MARLEY. To warn you.

(To audience.)

It is required of every man that the spirit within him should walk abroad among his fellowmen, and travel far and wide; and if that spirit goes not forth in life, it is condemned to do so (*to Scroogi*) after death.

SCROOGI. You are tie up with chain. Why is-a like dat?

MARLEY. I wear the chain I forged in life; I made it link by link, and yard by yard; I girded it on of my own free will, and of my own free will I wore it.

SCROOGI. It-a look-a good on you.

Music stops.

MARLEY. Thanks. Chains are all the rage in hell. Actually, everything's the rage in hell. There's wailing and gnashing of teeth.

SCROOGI. You're in hell?

MARLEY. I died, and I still inhabit the same plane of existence as Barton Street. If that's not hell, I don't know what is.

SCROOGI. That's-a grim... Grimsby news, Jacobi.

MARLEY. Oh, you haven't heard?

SCROOGI. Heard what?

MARLEY. Would you know the weight and length of the strong coil you bear yourself? It was full as heavy and as long as this, seven Christmas Eves ago. You have laboured on it, since. It is a ponderous chain!

SCROOGI. I got-a chain-a like that one?

MARLEY. Yes.

SCROOGI. Jacobi, old Jacobi Marlino, tell-a me some more. Make-a me feel-a more confortabile, Jacobi!

MARLEY. I'm all out of comfort.

SCROOGI. What-a you tell me!?

MARLEY. Comfort comes from other regions, Ebenezu Scroogi, and is conveyed by other ministers, to other kinds of men. Nor can I tell you what I would. A very little more is all permitted to me. I cannot rest or linger anywhere. My spirit never walked beyond our counting-house. Mark me!

GHOST (*Narrator 1, Hamlet's father*) Mark me!

Music stops.

MARLEY. Already haunted.

GHOST *(Narrator 1)*. Sorry.

Music: Carol of the Bells.

MARLEY. In life, my spirit never roved beyond the narrow limits of our money-changing hole, and weary journeys lie before me!

SCROOGI. Is that-a so bad? Ma, all-a da time you gooda man for businessi.

Music: organ.

MARLEY. Business! Mankind was my business. The common welfare was my business. The dealings of my trade were but a drop of water in the comprehensive ocean of my business!

Marley walks out into audience.

Why did I walk through crowds of fellow-beings with my eyes turned down, and never raise them to that blessed Star which led the Wise Men to a poor abode! Were there no poor homes to which its light would have conducted me?

SCROOGI. Take-a-easy, Jacob. No give-a me harda time-a, please.

Music: ominous, in a minor key.

MARLEY. I am here tonight to warn you that you have yet a chance and hope of escaping my fate. A chance and hope of my procuring, Ebenezu.

SCROOGI. You was all-a time-a my good-a friend, Jacob.

MARLEY. You will be visited by three spirits.

SCROOGI. Like-a da vino? Whiskey? Grappa?

MARLEY. No, ghosts.

SCROOGI. Dats-a my bigga chance? Madonna!

MARLEY. No, she can't come. She's on tour.

SCROOGI. That's-a too bad. She sing sweer. Three spiritu? I no like.

MARLEY. Without this, you can't escape my fate.

SCROOGI. Eh, Jacobi, I take-a all-a da ghost in-a one-a-time, and-a den everyt'ing-a finish fast.

MARLEY. No, you've got to take the ghosts one at a time. One hour apart. Preferably with meals. Side effects include low fever with nausea, stomach pain, and loss of appetite. Expect the first ghost when the bell tolls one.

SCROOGI. When it tolls one what?

MARLEY. Just when it tolls one-o'clock. That's all the time I've got, Ebenezu. I'm off to join the hordes of helpless shades doomed to wander the earth. Oh, uh... do you have bus-fare?

SCROOGI. I'm a little short.

MARLEY. That's alright, you're Sicilian. What did you expect?

He exits, his voice wailing in the distance.

MARLEY. What did you expe-e-e-ect?

SCROOGI. Ah... All an illusione! Bah, umba-!

Scroogi lies down and goes to sleep.

Music: Carol of the bells becoming weird.

3. Christmas Past

Ghost of Christmas Past (Holly) enters.

Music: Somewhere Over the Rainbow

Holly does a flying dance. When the music finishes the form, the Westminster Chimes boom out. Holly, startled, falls to the ground.

The bell tolls ONE. Scroogi jumps and cries out. The ghost is frightened again. She slaps SCROOGI.

HOLLY. Don't scare me like that!

SCROOGI. Signora, you da spiritu dat-a suppose to come-a to me?

HOLLY. I am.

SCROOGI. Who and-a what are you?

HOLLY. The Ghost of Christmas Past.

SCROOGI. Not-a da pasta. People no eat-a pasta at Chrissmiss time. Dey eat-a da goose and turkey.

HOLLY. I'm the Ghost of Christmases gone by.

SCROOGI. Gone buy? I gon' buy notting-a for Chrissimiss.

HOLLY. Pay attention!

SCROOGI. I no pay nobody if dey no work-a for me.

HOLLY. (*Explaining carefully.*) I'm a ghost.

SCROOGI. I know. You tell me.

HOLLY. I am the Ghost who represents Christmas during a time period which was prior to this moment.

SCROOGI. Oh! (*To audience.*) Why she no say that in-a first-a place?

HOLLY. *(To audience.)* This is the kind of dope you have to put up with in this line of work. *(To Scroogi.)* Look, just... call me Holly.

SCROOGI. You the ghost of-a long-a time past?

HOLLY. No. Your past.

SCROOGI. And why-a you here?

HOLLY. I'm doing a favour for Marley. I owe him.

SCROOGI. What he want to send-a you here for?

HOLLY. Your welfare.

SCROOGI. I no need welfare. I'm a rich-a man. I go back-a to bed now.

HOLLY. *(Sighs deeply.)* Your reclamation, then. Rise, and walk with me.

SCROOGI. You make-a mistake! You go to the window! No forget-a, I just-a flesh and blood. I can-a fall down.

HOLLY. Bear but a touch of my hand there, and you shall be upheld in more than this!

Music: Vitti Na Crozza

SCROOGI. Hamiltone... she's-a gone... where you take me?

HOLLY. You'll see.

SCROOGI. We go so fast. Is-a blue water everywhere. Is-a ocean, no?

HOLLY. That's right. Watch out.

SCROOGI. Where you take me?

HOLLY. Can't you guess?

SCROOGI. I see island. It's-a surround by bigga azzuro ocean. I know ... it's-a Sicilia.

HOLLY. Bingo.

Ensemble enters as Villagers, singing the refrain of Vitta Na Crozza.

> La la la lero
> La lero la lero
> La lero la lero
> La lero la la
>
> La la la lero
> La lero la lero
> La lero la lero
> La lero la la

Through the following, they hum the verse and sing the refrain.

SCROOGI. Madonna Mia! Dis-a where I live-a when I just-a boy! (*Pause.*) Dis-a Racalmuto.

There is-a da famosa fontanna. Is-a got-a spout for sweet water and-spout for-a bitter water. And da church, Santa Maria del Mondo, da famosa church-a where my momma and my poppa get-a married.

And my cousin, Salvatore, he deliver salt everywhere wit' a donkey. Lu sheku.

Everybody is-a farmer. But we no own-a da land. Da land belong-a to padrone, and we work-a like a sunamabeach, and da padrone take-a most everyt'ing-a. We gotta grow lots-a food, but we no keep. Most times to eat we just-a got onion and bread, meat only one, two time a year.

HOLLY. And Christmas?

SCROOGI. Chrissimiss time, everything about-a food. After da midnight mass, we go home, make-a fry sausage and we got-a canole, biscotti, and-a binulata and we play card-a game all night long, briscola, scopa.

Outside is-a damp-a and-a cold. So they burn-a da coal out-a side and when da coal is-a red hot, dey bring-a inside. And everybody sit down around da coal, and tell-a storia and make-a joke and drink vino and grappa.

And fo shu' we pray for when-a da tings are gonna be more better. We dream about America.

Ghost and Scroogi sing:

> Ce lu iardinu mezzu
> Di lu mari
> Chinu di limuni
> Arang' e scuri
> Tutti li giedri ci

Vannu a cantari
E li sireni beddri
Ci fannu amuri.

Sweet bitter Sicily
A land of love, a land of war,
Dark waves of history
Wash upon your golden shore
Children so full of dreams
Of brand new worlds beyond their door,
Farewell sweet Sicily
Until our hearts return to you once more.

La la la lero
La lero la lero
La lero la lero
La lero la la

La la la lero
La lero la lero
La lero la lero
La lero la la.

Racalmuto fades.

HOLLY. Come. There is more in your past.

They are inside a large hall.

HOLLY. Do you know this place?

SCROOGI. Fo shu', It's Hamiltone. I know dis-a place. There's old-a Don Fezziwiggi. He was my first-a boss in Canada!

FEZZIWIGGI is greeting guests at the party with double-cheek kisses. They're also kissing the rings on his hand.

Music: Love Theme from The Godfather.

SCROOGI. He live again! He die long-a time ago!

HOLLY. He seems nice.

SCROOGI. That's-a true, he seem-a nice.

HOLLY. He throws a really great party. What business is he in?

SCROOGI. Is-as no you business, that's-a what business he's in!

HOLLY. You can tell me. I'm a ghost!

SCROOGI. I tell you, and we both-a gonna be ghosts!

HOLLY. Can you tell me what you did for him?

ACT ONE   27

SCROOGI. My first-a jobba with Fezziwiggi is deliver the bottles for the sodapop to people. Ah, that Fezziwiggi! He got a bad-a side, but he look after the people. He look-a after me. Give-a me good-a job.

FEZZIWIGGI. Scroogi! Ebenezu! Come over here, say hello. Merry Christmas, Ebenezu. Here's something from your uncle Fezziwiggi.

(Fezziwiggi claps. One of his henchmen hands Scroogi a wad of money.)

FEZZIWIGGI. I'm good-a to you, Scroogi, so you be good-a to me.

SCROOGI. Thank you very much, Mr. Fezziwiggi.

FEZZIWIGGI. No, no. You familia. You call-a me Luigi. Come help Tio Fezziwiggi sing-a da song.

SCROOGI. Oh, Signore! Oh, Don Fezziwiggi. I no sing-a too good!

FEZZIWIGGI. You sing-a da song NOW!

Scroogi leads the cast and audience:

EH CUMPARI

Eh Cumpari, ci vuo sunari
E chi si sona lu friscalettu
E comu si sona lu friscalettu
(Whistle.)
Lu friscalettu, tipiti tipiti tam.
E cumpari, ci vo sunari
Chi si sona u viulinu
E comu si sona u viulinno
A zing a zing, u viulinu...
U friscalette, tipiti tipiti tam
guitarra ... stroma, stroma
trompetta ... toota toota

FEZZIWIGGI. (*To audience*) Time for you to get-a da drink. You get-a da drink NOW!

End of Act I

Act II

4. Belle

All enter singing. Fezziwiggi's party continues.

TU SCENDI DALLE STELLE

*Tu scendi dalle stelle,
O Re del Cielo,
e vieni in una grotta,
al freddo al gelo.
e vieni in una grotta,
al freddo al gelo.*

*O Bambino mio Divino
Io ti vedo qui a tremar,
O Dio Beato
Ahi, quanto ti costò
l'avermi amato!
Ahi, quanto ti costò
l'avermi amato!*

Belle sings:

> You came down from the stars
> Creator of heaven and earth,
> The angels did proclaim your
> Humble and holy birth.
> The angels did proclaim your
> Humble and holy birth.

All sing:

> O Bambino mio Divino
> Io ti vedo qui a tremar,
> O Dio Beato
> Ahi, quanto ti costò
> l'avermi amato!
> Ahi, quanto ti costò
> l'avermi amato!

Chorus exits, Belle, Scroogi and Holly remain.

SCROOGI. The first-a time I sing-a this song in Canada, that's-a when I see her. Her name was-a Belle. We meet-a me at the Fezziwiggi Chrissimiss party. She was-a my galafriend...

HOLLY. Was?

SCROOGI. Si, "was". You the Ghost of Chrissimiss Past. Everything-a is "was".

HOLLY. She was, I think, more than your girlfriend.

SCROOGI. Si. Si. I get-a more money when I work for Fezziwiggi. Is-a good money, so I ask-a Belle to marry me.

HOLLY. So, what happened with Belle?

SCROOGI. I no like-a to talk about what-a happen.

HOLLY. You're going to have to. Look who's here.

Belle approaches.

BELLE. It doesn't matter anymore. Another idol has displaced me.

SCROOGI. What-a t'ing-a more importante take-a you place?

BELLE. The only thing you put any importance on now: gold.

SCROOGI. Not-a just gold. There is other t'ing-a, too. Like-a money.

BELLE. You were so dear to me...and so you still are...but I am not dear to you. All you hold dear is money.

SCROOGI. But-a money make-a do world go round. Most hard ting-a is-a to be poor. And-a poor people, they no like-a people like-a me who got lots-a money.

BELLE. Everything you cared about has fallen away until that baser passion, Gain, has replaced them all.

SCROOGI. Whatta you talk about? Even if-a now I am-a more wise-a about money, that's-a nothing. I'm no change my feeling for you.

BELLE. You say that. Our engagement was made when we were both poor and content to be so.

SCROOGI. You t'ink I ask-a you to release-a me? When I tell-a you dat, huh?

BELLE. In words? Never.

SCROOGI. If-a no words, den what?

BELLE. In everything else. (*Pause.*) I release you. Goodbye... Ebenezu.

An instrumental version of Tu Scendi Dalle Stelle begins. Scroogi interrupts it.

SCROOGI. I hate-a dat song now! It's-a dead to me! Why you show-a me all-a dees sad-a tings!?

HOLLY. I didn't do this. You did.

Music: Carol of the Bells

SCROOGI. Leave me! Leave me!

HOLLY. What was Marley to you? What were Fezziwiggi and Belle to you? They were friends and loved ones! They loved you, Ebenezu Scroogi. So much love thrown to you! Thrown away!

SCROOGI. I can't take-a no more! GO!

HOLLY. And what were you to them? Nothing but a squeezing, wrenching, grasping, scraping, clutching, covetous, old sinner!

Ghost exits.

5. Christmas Present

BELLS toll two.

NATALIA. (*Off stage.*) Scroogi! Scroogi!

SCROOGI. Mamma mia!

NATALIA. (*Off Stage*) Scroogi! Scroogi! Get-a in here!

Ghost of Christmas Present (Natalia) enters.

NATALIA. Fine. I come-a to you.

SCROOGI. You one of those ghosts-a that come-a to haunt me and give-a me trouble?

NATALIA. That's-a right. You call me Natalia, the Ghost of Christmas Present.

SCROOGI. You my Christmas present? That's-a nice-a present.

NATALIA. Oh, my poor-a boy! You so skeeny, Scroogi! What-a you eat?

SCROOGI. Mio? I eat-a da polenta. It's-a good and-a cheap. Favoloso!

NATALIA. No! No! It's-a no good! You got to eat-a much better! Eat-a da turkey, and-a the stuffing, and-a molto, molto lasagna! Christmas lasagna! Get nice and round like-a Babbo Natale!

SCROOGI. But Babbo Natale, Santa Claus, he's-a no real! Dis kid come-a to sing when I work. I say to da kid, hey kid, there is no Santa Claus!

She smacks him.

SCROOGI. No, no! Take it easy! Take it easy!

NATALIA. You can't-a tell-a da children there is-a no Santa Claus! That's-a the mamma's job!

SCROOGI. Okay! Okay! Okay! It's alright! I no tell-a no more!

NATALIA. That's-a my good Scroogi!

She pats his head.

NATALIA. Now, come, my skinny little Scroogi!

SCROOGI. Spiritu, take-a me where you gotta take me.

NATALIA. That's-a my good-a Scroogi! Come! Hold on-a my hand!

SCROOGI. Where we go?

NATALIA. We go out into Christmas! What? You never been out-a on Christmas before?

SCROOGI. I work-a Chrissmiss time.

NATALIA. I take-a you. I show-a you Christmas. I show you is-a no umbaggo.

SCROOGI. But, it is a um…

NATALIA. Ah!

She smacks him.

NATALIA. Don't you talk-a back to me! Now we fly!

Music: Volare

SCROOGI. We fly across-a the ocean?

NATALIA. We gonna stay right here in Hamiltone. We fly downtown. We land on Stelco Tower. Look-a da beautiful Chrissimissi lights on da street and Gore Park, got-a nice decoration.

SCROOGI. You call-a downtown beautiful? Dey got-a building run down. Gore Park use to be bellissimo with real reindeer and lots-a kids playing, now just drunk people, people sell drug-a and lazaroni.

NATALIA. But da Jackson Mall got-a even more Chrissmiss decoration and-a people keep warm and-a dey be happy and-a shop.

SCROOGI. Natalia, you don't know nothing-a because you lost in-a da present. Jackson Mall just-a fill up-a with dollar store and-a junk-a. Where is Jackson Mall, use to be Eaton's with Santa Claus who give free candy and colouring books. In windows used to be puppets mechanical with beautiful Christmas scene. Now nothing-a. I no like-a downtown.

NATALIA. Okay, Scroogi, I take-a you to Bay Front-a. Look, look where people skate and have-a good time.

SCROOGI. Dats-a no good, like-a Vittoria Park use-a to be for skate. Dey play nice-a song for skate. Den you go to hot house for warm up beside wood stove and-a have fantastic-a hot chocolate.

NATALIA. Okay, okay. Let's go to see Chrissimiss party for people who work-a for Dofasco where-a Santa Clausi give-a kids-a nice present.

SCROOGI. Now maybe just-a Dofasco got-a Santa Clausi. In-a days before, use to be Santa Clausi in-a Westing-a-house-a, Stelco, National Steel Car. Everybody work-a and-a everybody get-a present. Now too many people is-a poor and dey getta drunk and use-a drug in Gore Park.

NATALIA. But even for poor kids, Chrissimiss is good-a day. Got a toy drive-a and-a more rich people be kind and give-a money. No like-a you. No like-a you! You just-a cheap and-a mean man.

SCROOGI. My money is-a my money, basta. Why you give-a me hard-a time?

NATALIA. I give-a you hard-a time because you got a hard-a head.

6. The Cratchits' Christmas

Music: O Tanenbaum

NATALIA. Oh...I know you recognise-a this place...!

SCROOGI. I never been-a here before.

NATALIA. Shame on you, my Scroogi! It's-a your clerk! Roberto! Roberto Cratchit! You never-a visit your clerk? How you gonna be a good-a boss?

SCROOGI. I don't want to be a good-a boss! I want to be a big-a boss.

NATALIA. Stronzo! Just-a watch.

Cratchit and Tiny Tim are on their way home. Mrs. Cratchit is making dinner.

CRATCHIT. Is that dinner I smell? Tim, I said is that dinner I smell?

TINY TIM. Boy, I hope not!

CRATCHIT. Tim! That's your mother's cooking you're talking about.

TINY TIM. Oh! It's my mother's cooking?

CRATCHIT. Yes.

TINY TIM. Oh! Uh, I mean...mmmm! That smells...unique.

CRATCHIT. Sh! Don't upset your mother.

TINY TIM. We should cheer her up.

CRATCHIT: That's a lovely idea, Tiny Tim, how are we going to do that?

TINY TIM: Uh... can you juggle?

CRATCHIT: No.

TINY TIM: Can you... dance?

CRATCHIT: Not really, no.

TINY TIM: What can you do?

CRATCHIT: Uh, well... I work in accounts for Mr. Scrugi.

TINY TIM: Oh, good, dad. We'll cheer mom up with your robust knowledge of polynomial equations.

CRATCHIT: Don't be sarcastic.

TINY TIM: Who's being sarcastic?

Cratchit and Tiny Tim enter their house.

MRS. CRATCHIT. I thought I heard voices!

TINY TIM. She's hearing voices! Run for your lives, she's going nuts! Save yourself!

SCRUGI: (*To Natalia*) This is no what I expect. This is no Leave It To Beaver.

MRS. CRATCHIT. How was church?

TINY TIM. Everybody kept looking at me.

CRATCHIT. Don't you want them to remember, on Christmas, who made lame men walk and blind men see?

TINY TIM. Sure, but they can do that without staring at me.

MRS. CRATCHIT. Come my dear. Let's sit down to dinner! I'll bring out the turkey.

Mrs. C. brings in scrawny little rubber turkey on plate.

MRS. CRATCHIT. Tah-dah! The turkey!

TINY TIM. That's a turkey?

CRATCHIT. Oh my dear, you've outdone yourself.

TINY TIM. Hashtag: low standards.

CRATCHIT seats TIM.

MRS. CRATCHIT pulls him aside.

MRS. CRATCHIT. How is he?

CRATCHIT. He's growing very strong and healthy, my dear.

SCROOGI. What's-a happen here?

NATALIA. That's-a called foreshadowing!

CRATCHIT. And now, before we eat the turkey! A toast!

MRS. CRATCHIT: I'll get the Christmas cheer.

TINY TIM: Oh, alcohol!

CRATCHIT: That's not for you, you little dickens.

Mrs. Cratchit brings tiny wine glasses.

CRATCHIT: A Merry Christmas to us all, my dears. God bless us!

ALL. Merry Christmas! Bless us!

TINY TIM. God bless us! Every one!

CRATCHIT. That's very nice, Tiny Tim.

TINY TIM. Except for Donald Trump.

(He has trouble pronouncing "Trump".)

CRATCHIT. No! No! Tim, that's not a nice word for a ventroliquist.

TINY TIM. Neither is Donald Trump.

CRATCHIT. Tim!

TINY TIM. Bob!

SCROOGI. Spiritu, Tiny Tim, he gonna live or he gonna die?

NATALIA. Oh, my Scroogi… I see-a twitter feed with no tweets, and a cell-a phone that's gone cold.

SCROOGI. That's-a no clear for me.

NATALIA. What? I got-a spell it all out for you?

SCROOGI. I no even speak English. You think I can spell?

NATALIA. Is okay, Scroogi! You don't have to be smart! I still love you!

SCROOGI. What? I'm-a not smart?

NATALIA. You got-a no friends, you don't talk to your famiglia, and all you do is save up-a your money so you make a nice-a rich-a corpse. You not gonna win-a da blue ribbon for your brains, that's-a fo' sure.

ACT TWO 39

MRS. CRATCHIT. Are you feeling better, Tiny Tim?

TINY TIM. I think so... did you make dessert, too?

MRS. CRATCHIT. Of course! I'll bring it out right now!

TINY TIM. Oh, good, mom! I can't wait!

CRATCHIT. While we wait for dessert...

TINY TIM. ... for our doom.

CRATCHIT. Why don't you sing for us, Tim?

TINY TIM. I'm playing Pokemon.

CRATCHIT. Please?

TINY TIM. I'd rather die.

Mrs. Cratchit brings tiny desert.

SCROOGI. So, Tiny Tim... that's-a foreshadowing too? Tiny Tim is-a gonna die?

NATALIA. (*Big sigh.*) I see-a twitter feed with no tweets, and a cell phone that's gone cold...

SCROOGI. You already tell me this.

NATALIA. If this-a visione not-a change, he gonna die. That make-a sense to you now? Oh, my poor, poor, stupido Scroogi...

SCROOGI. No, no! You good spiritu. Tell-a me he gonna live.

NATALIA. Okay, if it make-a you feel better. He gonna live.

SCROOGI. That's-a fo shu'?

NATALIA. Nope. He's-a gonna die. But, so what? If-a he like-a to die, den let-a die. Make-a da population more small. Too much-a people, anyway.

SCROOGI is silent.

CRATCHIT. I'll give you Mr. Scroogi, the Founder of the Feast!

MRS. CRATCHIT. The Founder of the Feast, indeed! I wish I had him here. I'd give him a piece of my mind.

CRATCHIT. My dear! Christmas Day!

MRS. CRATCHIT. Since it's Christmas, I am to drink the health of such an odious, stingy, hard, unfeeling man as Mr. Scroogi! You know he is, Robert. Nobody knows it better than you do, poor fellow!

TINY TIM. I'm with Mom on this one.

MRS. CRATCHIT. A Merry Christmas, Mr; Scroogi.

TINY TIM. *(Makes raspberry noise.)*

Cratchit and Mrs C. exit.

7. Fred's Christmas

Nephew Fred, his wife Catherine, Guest 1 (man) and Guest 2 (woman) enter singing:

I SAW THREE SHIPS COME SAILING IN

*I saw three ships come sailing in,
On Christmas day, on Christmas day,
I saw three ships come sailing in,
On Christmas day in the morning.*

*And what was in those ships all three?
On Christmas day, on Christmas day,
And what was in those ships all three?
On Christmas day in the morning.*

*Our Saviour Christ and his lady,
On Christmas day, on Christmas day,
Our Saviour Christ and his lady,
On Christmas day in the morning.*

*And all the bells on earth shall ring,
On Christmas day, on Christmas day,
And all the bells on earth shall ring,
On Christmas day in the morning.*

FRED. He said that Christmas was a humbug! He believed it too!

CATHARINE. More shame for him, Fred.

FRED. He's a comical old fellow, that's the truth, and not so pleasant as he might be. But, who suffers by his ill whims? Himself, always. Here he takes it into his head to dislike us, and he won't come and dine with us. What's the consequence? He don't lose much of a dinner.

FRED laughs.

CATHARINE. Indeed! I think he loses a very good dinner!

CATHARINE laughs, too.

ALL. Yes! A wonderful dinner! Don't let him off easy, Catharine.

NATALIA. Oh! You hear that-a man! He make-a fun of his wife's-a cooking!

FRED. How about a game?

CATHARINE. Does everyone know "The Minister's Cat"!

GUEST 1. No, no! Let's do Scroogi's cat!

The guests clap their hands and take turns thinking of words in alphabetical order that describe Scroogi's cat. A player who can't think of a word drops out. Scroogi becomes annoyed with the negative qualities associated with his fictitious cat, and tries to insert his own alternatives.

There is a simple, rhythmic musical accompaniment.

FRED. Scroogi's cat is an awful cat.

GUEST 1. Scroogi's cat is a bad cat

GUEST 2. Scroogi's cat is a cheap cat.

SCROOGI. Is a charming cat.

CATHERINE. Scroogi's cat is a disagreeable cat.

FRED. Scroogi's cat is an egocentric cat.

GUEST 1. Scroogi's cat is a f..f...f... (*He falters.*)

SCROOGI. Fantastic cat!

GUEST 1. I'm out.

They start again.

GUEST 2. Scroogi's cat is a finicky cat.

CATHERINE. Scroogi's cat is a grouchy cat.

FRED. Scroogi's cat is a haughty...

SCROOGI. Humble!

FRED. ... cat.

GUEST 2. Scroogi's cat is an ignorant cat.

CATHERINE. Scroogi's cat is a jerky cat.

SCROOGI. Jolly cat!

FRED. Scroogi's cat is a kooky cat.

GUEST 2. Scroogi's cat is a... (*She can't think of a word.*)

SCROOGI. A lovely cat!

They start again. Now it is just Catherine and Fred, face to face.

CATHERINE. Scroogi's cat is a loathsome cat.

FRED. Scroogi's cat is a miserly cat.

SCROOGI. A modest cat.

CATHERINE. Scroogi's cat is a nasty, no-good for nothing cat.

SCROOGI. A nice cat.

FRED. Scroogi's cat is an obnoxious cat.

SCROOGI. An okay cat.

CATHERINE. Scroogi's cat is a putrid, pigheaded, penny-pinching pussycat.

FRED. Scroogi's cat is a quarrelsome cat.

CATHERINE. Scroogi's cat is a ridiculous cat.

SCROOGI. Why they no like-a my cat?

FRED. Scroogi's cat is a stingy old cat.

CATHERINE. Scroogi's cat is a tightfisted old tightwad cat.

FRED. Scroogi's cat is an ugly, unkind, unsavory, ungenerous cat.

SCROOGI. Unusually nice cat!

CATHERINE. Scroogi's cat is a villainous cat.

SCROOGI. A very nice cat!

FRED. Scroogi's cat is a weird cat.

SCROOGI. A wonderfully nice cat!

CAHTERINE. Scroogi's cat is . . . is . . . is . . . I can't think of one with *x*.

Music stops.

SCROOGI. An *x*-tremely nice cat.

CATHARINE. I don't think it was Scroogi's cat. I think we were talking about Scroogi!

FRED. Well, he's a good sport, even though he isn't here!

GUEST 2. He's a good sport because he isn't here!

FRED. Well, it would be ungrateful not to drink his health.

The musical accompanyment starts again, as the guests exit, singing:

Scroo-oo-oo-gi
Scroo-oo-oo-gi
Scroo-oo-oo-gi

SCROOGI. Okay! Everybody have-a fun! Where we go now?

NATALIA. Me? I go nowhere no more.

SCROOGI. What-a you mean?

NATALIA. I go away. Is-a present-a no more.

SCROOGI. Eh! The life-a of a spiritu is like-a dat, short?

NATALIA. I am only for the present. No more. Is too much. You want-a too much from-a you poor-a Natalia. I go away at end of tonight-a!

SCROOGI. But you my Chrissimiss present! You no can stay? Madonna Mia!

NATALIA. Eh! Watch-a you mouth!

ACT TWO 45

SCROOGI. Scuse! Scuse!

NATALIA. That's-a better! That's-a my Scroogi! You wait here. I come back.

Speaking towards off-stage.

Come now, bambinos! Come with Natalia!

Natalia gets puppets: Ignorance (a girl) and Want (a boy).

Sombre music.

SCROOGI. Spiritu, dis-a you kids-a?

NATALIA. No. These? They belong-a to you.

SCROOGI. Oh, no! I'm-a good-a boy!

NATALIA. No, no, no! Not-a to you alone! They are belong-a to mankind! And they take after their pappa and mamma. But they cling-a to me for protection!

This is Ignorance. This is Want. You look out for them both, but most for this-a boy!

SCROOGI. But... but, dey gotta no place to live? No money for to live?

NATALIA. Eh? Whatsa matta? They got-a no jail on-a Barton Street? No welfare?

Natalie exits with Ignorance and Want.

NATALIA. (*Her voice fading away*) They got-a no jail on-a Barton Street? No welfare?

8. What Is To Come?

An ominous version of Carol of the Bells, as Scroogi lies down and goes to sleep.

Westminster chimes. Clock strikes three.

The Ghost of Christmas Future enters. She is a silent ghost in a fright wig.

SCROOGI. Dis-a be the Spiritu of da Chrissimissi of da futuro, that's-a gonna come?

GHOST honks a horn at her waist. One honk for YES.

SCROOGI. That's-a "yes"?

GHOST honks once.

SCROOGI. Well, let's-a see what-a you wanna show me. I know dis-a for my own good. We gonna fly? (*Honks twice, NO.*) We gonna drive? (*Honks twice.*) We gonna take the LRT? (*Honks twice.*) There's-a no LRT? (*Honks twice.*) This future she's no look-a too good. What we gonna do? (*Ghost mimes walking.*) Let's a-walk.

Music: Feliz Navidad Walking Music.

They arrive at the pawn shop.

Music: Jingle Bell Rock.

SCROOGI. (*To Ghost*) What's-a this place? (*Ghost does not reply.*) You no say no t'ing-a?

PAWNBROKER. (*To Ghost*) Hey, you! (*Ghosts honks.*)

SCROOGI. He can-a see us…? (*Ghost honks.*)

PAWNBROKER. (*To Scroogi*) You? You know anything about money?

SCROOGI. It's-a what I spend-a my life to get.

PAWNBROKER. If you spend your life to get the money, what are you gonna spend the money on?

SCROOGI. I get-a but I no spend.

ACT TWO 47

PAWNBROKER. I'm having trouble accounting.

SCROOGI. Well, dat's-a easy! I know all about-a counting.

PAWNBROKER. I wish you'd explain it to me.

SCROOGI. She's-a go like dis: one-a, two, t'ree...all-a way up.

PAWNBROKER. One, two, three... What comes after three?

SCROOGI. Ma, four-a.

PAWNBROKER. What's after four?

SCROOGI. Five-a.

PAWNBROKER. What's after five?

SCROOGI. That's a supper time. Mangia-mangia.

Charwoman enters with a big bag. She is a classic pantomime Dame.

PAWNBROKER. Uh-oh. More trouble.

CHARWOMAN. Can you see me now?

PAWNBROKER. Yeah, but I can't figure out what I did to deserve it.

CHARWOMAN. My boss died just yesterday...

PAWNBROKER. He couldn't just fire you?

CHARWOMAN. ... and I have some items that you might be interested in.

PAWNBROKER. Oh, really?

PAWNBROKER. Beat it, you two, I think she's serious.

CHARWOMAN. They can stay.

PAWNBROKER. I didn't know you were that kinda girl.

SCROOGI. Spiritu, I t'ink-a I know her... I think-a I know her... I know you from-a someplace...

48   SCROOGISSIMO

CHARWOMAN. Who's this?

PAWNBROKER. He was helping me with my figures. Maybe you'd like him to take a look at your figure; you could use the help. On second thought, I don't think there's any help for you; you're a lost cause. Don't get me wrong, I've got nothing against your body, it's just, well, let's keep it that way.

CHARWOMAN. I've got some items from the dear departed.

PAWNBROKER. Never a truer phrase spoken! He's only dear now that he's departed. I can see why you worked for him – birds of a feather flock together.

SCROOGI. I know! I got it! She's-a my cleaning woman! (*To the Charwoman.*) You clean-a my house!

CHARWOMAN. 'Ere! I don't take orders from you! Don't come near me!

PAWNBROKER. I don't think you'll have to tell him twice. So, what do you got for me?

CHARWOMAN. Here. (*Puts the bag on the table.*)

PAWNBROKER. Very nice, very nice. So, you want me to buy this bag?

CHARWOMAN. No! This bag is me own.

PAWNBROKER. I'll give you a dollar for it.

CHARWOMAN. That's an insult!

PAWNBROKER. (*To Scroogi.*) What do you think? A dollar for the bag?

SCROOGI. You gotta pay me more den one dollar to take-a dis bag offa you hands.

PAWNBROKER. All right, I've decided! You can keep the bag, I don't want it after all. What else you got?

CHARWOMAN. These are his bedcurtains.

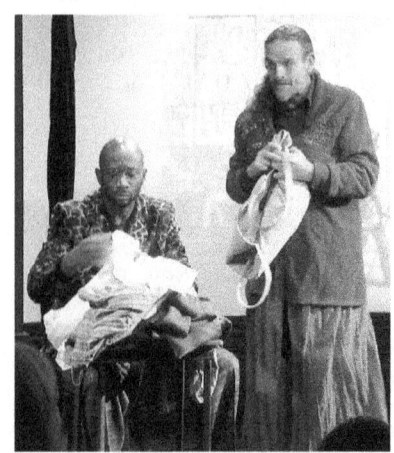

SCROOGI. Those-a look-a like my bed curtains!

PAWNBROKER. I'll give you a dollar for that.

CHARWOMAN. I'm not done! I've got his blanket, too.

ACT TWO   49

PAWNBROKER. You took this with him lying there?

CHARWOMAN. I did. Got his pyjamas, too.

PAWNBROKER. You took the pyjamas right off a dead man!

CHARWOMAN. What if I did?

PAWNBROKER. He'll catch cold!

CHARWOMAN. If he wanted to keep 'em after he was dead, the wicked old screw, why wasn't he nice in his lifetime? If he had been, he'd have had somebody to look after him when he was struck with Death, instead of lying gasping out his last, there alone by himself. It's a judgment on him.

SCROOGI. Spiritu! I got-a the curtains just-a like-a dat... Who die-a like this? All alone, nobody to help, nobody to care, nobody to show him love...

PAWNBROKER. (*To CHARWOMAN*) Here's the total. I always give too much to the ladies, it's a weakness of mine. Especially the pretty ones.

CHARWOMAN. This isn't good enough by half.

PAWNBROKER. Well, you're not one of the pretty ones. Take it or leave it. Actually, just take it and leave.

CHARWOMAN. I suppose I take what I can, and thank you kindly. It's more generous than he ever was to me, I'm sure.

Charwoman takes back empty bag.

PAWNBROKER. What are you two still doing here?

Scroogi and the Ghost show the Pawnbroker a poster from the show.

PAWNBROKER. Oh, this is your show? Well, pardon me!

Pawnbroker exits.

SCROOGI. Spiritu, I can't take-a this thing. This-a man, nobody feel-a sorry for him. He die, but nobody be sad.

I know this-a might-a be me. I learn-a my lesson.

Show me some-a comfort, Spiritu. Show me when some-a people die, people remember him wit' a kind-a heart.

They walk, then stop to observe the next interaction.

Cratchit enters to gloomy music, with Tiny Tim on a gurney. He tries to revive Tiny Tim, giving him artificial respiration, electric shock, CPR etc. He gives up, takes a handkerchief from his pocket and covers the puppet. He picks up the handkerchief, wipes his eyes, and replaces it. He pushes the gurney offstage.

SCROOGI. No, no, no...please, spiritu, no! No Tiny Tim! Dat's-a no comfort! I can take-a no more! Tiny-a Tim! Why, Spiritu? Why is-a like this?

The Ghost points to the front of the stage.

SCROOGI. What'a you do? You show me graveyard! A grave-a stone.

The Ghost continues to point.

SCROOGI. Okay...but, Spiritu...before I go to look-a at dis-a stone-a, I gotta ask a questione... These things dat's-a gonna happen fo shu', or things that's gonna happen maybe? I can change dis-a t'ing, si?

Ghost exits. Scroogi moves forward to look at the gravestone.

SCROOGI. Dat's-a my name! Dat's-a my name! Ebenezu Scroogi, Stronzo Numero Uno! Numero Uno? No Numero du', or t'ree? People gonna come forever, they gonna see dis... No! Spiritu! Tell me how I can-a take-a these words off-a dis tombstone. I gotta make-a t'ings change? Tell-a me how I can-a take-a my name off-a dis stone! Please! It's-a my name! It's-a my name!

9. Christmas Day

Fred, Cratchit, Three Fundraisers enter singing:

HERE WE COME A-WASSAILING

Here we come a-wassailing among the leaves so green;
Here we come a-wandering, so fair to be seen.
Love and joy come to you, and to you our wassail, too.
And God bless you and send you a Happy New Year,
And God send you a Happy New Year.

We are not daily beggars that beg from door to door;
But we are neighbours' children whom you have seen before.
Love and joy come to you, and to you our wassail, too.
And God bless you and send you a Happy New Year,
And God send you a Happy New Year.

Scroogi is standing stage right.

SCROOGI. I not dead-a yet-a! No morto! No morto! Oh Jacobi Marlino! Grazie! Grazie, Jacobi! I'm-a gonna go to my knee, amigo Jacobi, I fall-a on my knee. I feel so light, I could fly. I got-a no idea what-a day or month is-a today. I don't know how long I be wit da ghost. I no understand-a nothing-a.

FUNDRAISER 1. Mr Scroogi?

FUNDRAISER 2. Ebenezu Scroogi!

FUNDRAISER 3. Don't attract his attention! Let's get out of here!

SCROOGI. My good-a friend-a. How you do? I hope-a you make-a big money yesterday. You very kind-a people. Merry Chrissimissi to you! I got-a somet'ing for you!

He hands a wad of bills.

FUNDRAISER 1. You're joking.

FUNDRAISER 2. You're joking.

FUNDRAISER 3. You're joking.

SCROOGI. I no-a joke. So many years I be very cheap-a man. Now come-a time to be generoso.

FUNDRAISER 3. I don't know what to...

FUNDRAISER 2. ... this is so... Merry Christmas!

FUNDRAISER 1. Merry Christmas!

> *God bless the master of this house, likewise the mistress, too;*
> *And all the little children that round the table go.*
> *Love and joy come to you, and to you our wassail, too.*
> *And God bless you and send you a Happy New Year*
> *And God send you a Happy New Year*

Fundraiser 3 becomes the Little Girl during last verse.

All others sit on bench.

SCROOGI. Eh! Eh, you-a! Kid! What-a day she be today?

LITTLE GIRL. You're mean.

SCROOGI. No, no! No more mean! I'm-a change.

LITTLE GIRL. You told me there was no Santa Claus.

SCROOGI. Oh. That's-a right. Hey kid, what be your name?

LITTLE GIRL. Virginia.

SCROOGI. Yes, Virginia, there IS a Santa Claus!

LITTLE GIRL. There is?

SCROOGI. There gotta be. There's a spiritu, there's a ghost. Gotta be a Santa Claus. Tell me, what day she be today?

KID. It's Christmas Day!

SCROOGI. It's-a Chrissimiss Day. Eh I no miss Chrissimis. I still gotta time!

Here, take-a this money and go down to the shop-a down the street. Butcher store. And-a buy the more big-a turkey you see! The one big-a like you!

KID. You can't get a turkey on Christmas Day.

SCROOGI. Close? Mincha. (*He ponders.*) Keep the money. Is all right. Keep-a da money.

(*The Little Girl exits joyously.*)

SCROOGI. Store is close? Hmm. I know what I gotta do. I make-a one-a phone call.

(*He takes out his cell phone. Theme from the Godfather starts.*)

SCROOGI. Guido?   It's-a Ebenezu. Yeah, Scroogi. Buon Natale a te e alla tua famiglia. I need a favore. I like-a for you to go to the house of-a dis guy, he work-a for me, his name is Bob-a Cratchit. I want for you to go to his house... His shoe size? No. NO! NO! Shoe size, no. Is-a no that kind of favore!

I need-a for you to get-a for me a big-a turkey. Turkey! Yeah! You bring a turkey to dis-a guy, on-a Barton Street. 987 Barton Street. Hey, Guido. You bring-a in a limosine. You let him see the limosine. Si, si. No shoe size! Turkey! Buon Natale.

(*He chuckles.*)

SCROOGI. You gotta know the right-a people. (*Exits.*)

Fred and Catherine's party. The guests sing:

SILENT NIGHT

Silent night! Holy night!
All is calm, all is bright.
Round yon Virgin Mother and Child,
Holy infant so tender and mild,
Sleep in Heavenly peace!
Sleep in Heavenly peace!

Silent night! Holy night!
Shepherds quake at the sight...

During the first verse, Scroogi has put on his coat and hat, and now appears at the entrance to the party. Fred catches sight of him and moves towards him. The singing falls silent.

Scroogi extends his hand. Fred shakes it. Then he embraces his uncle.

In silence, Fred invites Catherine to welcome Scroogi. She hesitates while Scroogi waits in uncertainty. Then she smiles and embraces him. The piano finishes the verse, while she brings him in to join the group.

Scroogi greets each of the guests, while they sing:

> *Silent night! Holy night!*
> *Shepherds quake at the sight.*
> *Glories stream from Heaven afar,*
> *Heavenly hosts sing Alleluia,*
> *Christ, the Saviour, is born!*
> *Christ, the Saviour, is born!*

The others exit quietly, as Scroogi sings:

> *Notte sacro*
> *Silencioso*
> *Tutt' e calma*
> *Luminoso*
> *Madre vergine e divino*
> *Tenere mite Jesu bambino*
> *Dorme in pace del mondo*
> *Dormi in pace Jesu.*

10. As Good as His Word

Scroogi goes to his office, full of glee, and decorates.

Cratchit approaches the office, carrying Tiny Tim.

CRATCHIT. Oh! I'm late! I slept in!

TINY TIM. It's all that tripophan in the turkey.

CRATCHIT. Mr. Scroogi is going to kill me!

TINY TIM. We'll get your insurance money.

CRATCHIT. I can't afford life insurance.

TINY TIM. That's very irresponsible.

CRATCHIT. I work hard to support you and your mother.

TINY TIM. If you work so hard, why are you so late?

CRATCHIT. That's not a very helpful attitude.

TINY TIM. You're still going to get fired.

CRATCHIT enters the shop.

SCROOGI. Why you come-a late today? What's-a matta you?

CRATCHIT. I'm very sorry, sir. I'm very sorry I'm late.

SCROOGI. Dats-a fo shu' you late.

TINY TIM. That's because he overslept.

CRATCHIT. You're not helping.

SCROOGI. You bring-a you boy?

CRATCHIT. It's Bring your Child to Work Day.

TINY TIM. I'm being punished.

SCROOGI. Come-a more close, per favore.

TINY TIM. Here it comes.

SCROOGI. I gonna say one-a thing importante, amico mio.

CRATCHIT. It was Christmas, sir.

SCROOGI. Every year you make-a merry on-a Christmas, and I don't-a make merry on Christmas. That's-a gonna happen-a no more! Capische?

CRATCHIT. Yes sir.

TINY TIM. You are so fired.

SCROOGI. So, is-a time-a for me to start-a make-a merry... with you!

CRATCHIT. You feeling alright, sir?

TINY TIM. Oh, no! He's just as nuts as the rest of them.

SCROOGI. And you come-a late. I'm gonna change your pay. You pay, she's-a gonna go... up! More money for a job-a.

TINY TIM. He's a real screwball!

CRATCHIT. Sir, did you bump your head?

SCROOGI. If I hit-a my head, it's make-a me more smart. Not just-a pay. You gonna get-a benefit: pensione, index-a to cost-a da living. Dentist! You got teeth you gotta fix, you go to dentist. Maybe you gonna get a massage. Vacation.

And Tiny Tim, he's got this old-a cell phone. No more! Dis here is a present for Tiny Tim. One-a minut', I gotta take out some number. Okay, is ready now. And we-a gonna go to lunch and talk about everyt'ing is gonna change. Bob, turn up-a da heat. Because you no gonna work in this cold place for a cold boss no more! And-a dats fo' shu'.

CRATCHIT. Did you hear that, Tiny Tim?

TINY TIM. I sure did. God Bless us every one.

CRATCHIT. Except who?

TINY TIM. Except nobody! God bless us everyone!

The rest of the cast enters. All sing:

WE WISH YOU A MERRY CHRISTMAS

We wish you a Merry Christmas.
We wish you a Merry Christmas.
We wish you a Merry Christmas
And a Happy New Year.

Good tidings we bring
For you and your kin,
Good tidings for Christmas
And a Happy New Year.

So bring us some figgy pudding
So bring us some figgy pudding
So bring us some figgy pudding
And a cup of good cheer.

We won't go until we get some
We won't go until we get some
We won't go until we get some
So bring it right here.

We wish you a happy Chunnakah
We wish you a happy Kwanza
We wish you a Merry Christmas
And a Happy New Year.

Reprise: Eh Cumpari

And all exit singing Lu, Lu, Lu...

www.ingramcontent.com/pod-product-compliance
Lightning Source LLC
Chambersburg PA
CBHW051716040426
42446CB00008B/914